354696

Where is my School?

Written by Alison Sage

Collins

D1323491

This is my table.

Michael

Maisie

Nico

Leah sits next to me.

This is my classroom.

our plant

My teacher's name is Miss Salim.

our computer

our lunch boxes

This is my school.

the hall

the playground

my classroom

7

My school is in London.

I go to school with Mum.

I go to school on a bus.

London is in England.

Edinburgh

Belfast

UNITED

S

NORTHERN
IRELAND

England is part of the United Kingdom.

AND

KINGDOM

ENGLAND

ES

Cardiff

London

The United Kingdom is on Earth.

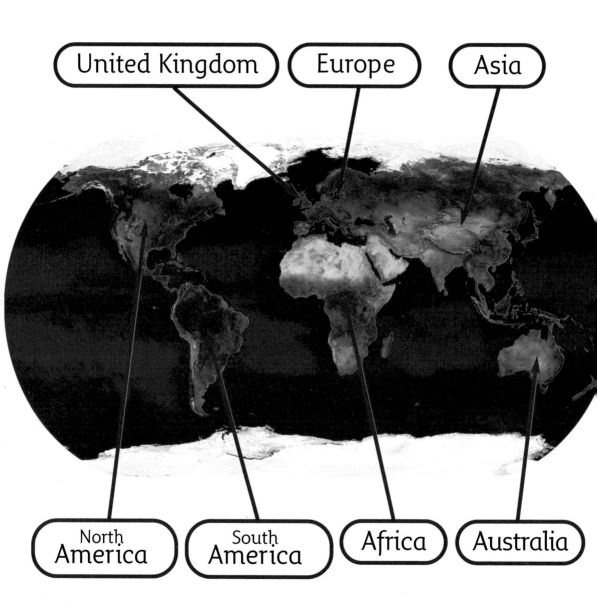

United Kingdom

Europe

Asia

North America

South America

Africa

Australia

Earth is in space.

My school is here.
Where is your school?

United Kingdom

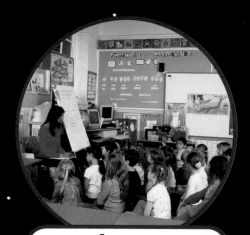

London

my school

my classroom

Index

🐾 Ideas for guided reading 🐾

Learning objectives: to read and use labels; to read high frequency words; to recognise the shape and length of more difficult words; to find words within these words; to ask and answer questions.

Curriculum links: Geography: Around my school; Where in the world is Barnaby Bear?

High frequency words: this, is, my, to, next, me, school, in, go, with, mum, here, of, the, on, where, your

Interest words: classroom, teacher, London, England, United Kingdom, Earth, space

Word Count: 63

Resources: atlases, globe

Getting started

- Look at the cover and read the title with the children. Discuss what the book might be about.

- Walk through the book looking at the photographs and labels up to p13. Ask the children where the school is. Is this near their school?

- Ask whether they have ever taken a photo. Then ask the children what they notice about the photos in the book. Elicit the response that the camera is further and further away in each photo – the later photos are taken from outer space.

- Point out examples of more difficult words, e.g. *London, England, United Kingdom, Earth, space* (pp10–13). Read each word and ask each child to find it in the book. They could look for words within a word, e.g. *London* (on), and *England* (and).

Reading and responding

- Ask the children to read the book independently. Observe, prompt and praise for reading with finger-pointing only at points of difficulty. Encourage them to read the labels as well as the main text. If any finish early, ask them to read all the labels again carefully.

- Read pp14–15 together. Ask the children what these photos show. Talk about photos taken from the air or space. Can they see the school in these? Discuss what else the photos show.

FALKIRK COUNCIL
LIBRARY SUPPORT
FOR SCHOOLS